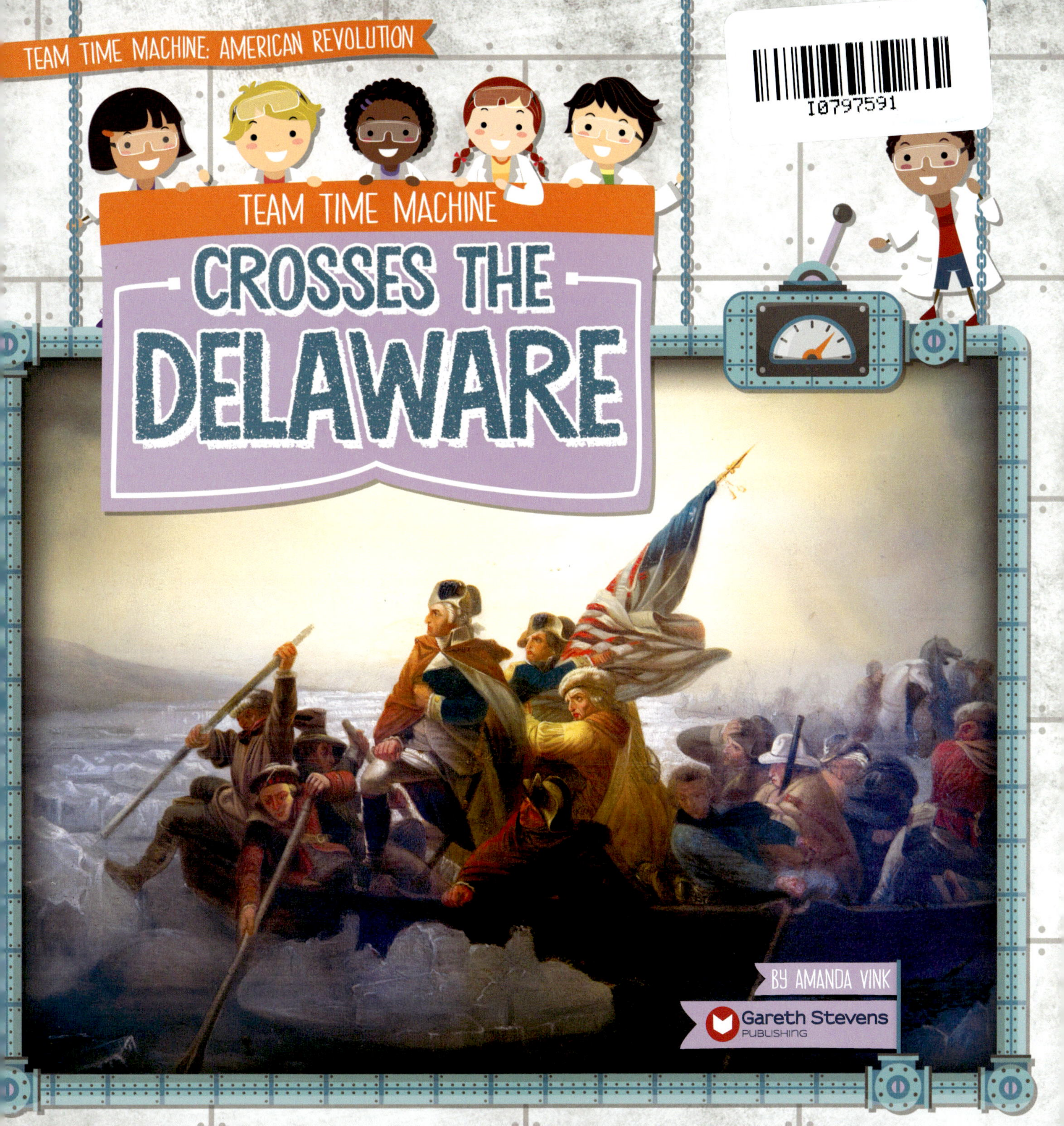
TEAM TIME MACHINE: AMERICAN REVOLUTION
TEAM TIME MACHINE
CROSSES THE
DELAWARE
BY AMANDA VINK
Gareth Stevens
PUBLISHING

Please visit our website, www.garethstevens.com. For a free color catalog of all our high-quality books, call toll free 1-800-542-2595 or fax 1-877-542-2596.

Library of Congress Cataloging-in-Publication Data

Names: Vink, Amanda, author.
Title: Team time machine crosses the Delaware / Amanda Vink.
Description: New York : Gareth Stevens Publishing, 2020. | Series: Team time machine: American Revolution | Includes index.
Identifiers: LCCN 2019009004| ISBN 9781538246740 (pbk.) | ISBN 9781538246764 (library bound) | ISBN 9781538246757 (6 pack)
Subjects: LCSH: United States–History–Revolution, 1775-1783–Juvenile literature.
Classification: LCC E208 .V68 2020 | DDC 973.3–dc23
LC record available at https://lccn.loc.gov/2019009004

First Edition

Published in 2020 by
Gareth Stevens Publishing
111 East 14th Street, Suite 349
New York, NY 10003

Designer: Katelyn E. Reynolds
Editor: Therese Shea

Photo credits: Cover, p. 1 Visions of America/UIG via Getty Images; cover, pp. 1–24 (series characters) Lorelyn Medina/Shutterstock.com; cover, pp. 1–24 (time machine elements) Agor2012/Shutterstock.com; cover, pp. 1–24 (background texture) somen/Shutterstock.com; p. 5 Thiranun Kunatum/Shutterstock.com; p. 7 courtesy of the Library of Congress; p. 9 United States Army (https://www.army.mil/e2/-images/2009/08/23/48245/) U.S. Army Center of Military History, The American Soldier series: Set 3. CMH Pub 70-1-3./Creuzbourg/Wikipedia.org; p. 11 Hulton Archive/Getty Images; p. 13 Washington-Custis-Lee Collection, Washington and Lee University, Lexington, Virginia And at (http://www.americanmilitaryhistorymsw.com/blog/536357-washingtons-mission)/Hohum/Wikipedia.org; p. 15 APPER/Wikipedia.org; pp. 17, 18 Andrew F. Kazmierski/Shutterstock.com; p. 19 The Metropolitan Museum of Art (https://www.metmuseum.org/collections/search-the-collections/20011777)/Aavindraa/Wikipedia.org; p. 21 (main) The Print Collector/Print Collector/Getty Images; p. 21 (map) Rainer Lesniewski/Shutterstock.com; p. 23 Joe Sohm/Visions of America/UIG via Getty Images; p. 25 Stock Montage/Getty Images; p. 27 Ann Ronan Pictures/Print Collector/Getty Images; p. 29 PAUL J. RICHARDS/AFP/Getty Images.

Printed in the United States of America

CONTENTS

WORDS IN THE GLOSSARY APPEAR IN **BOLD** TYPE THE FIRST TIME THEY ARE USED IN THE TEXT.

CHAPTER 1: A CHRISTMAS TRADITION

"What are you doing over holiday break?" Sam asked.

"My mom wants to take me to Trenton, New Jersey," answered Ben.

"What's there?" asked Mia.

"It's where George Washington crossed the Delaware River," Ben said. "Every year, they act out what happened."

"It has something to do with the American **Revolution**, when people in the American colonies wanted freedom from England," said Sam.

"Let's find out more!" said Mia. She took off running for the library. Sam and Ben were close behind.

MEET TEAM TIME MACHINE

TEAM TIME MACHINE IS A GROUP OF FRIENDS WHO FOUND A TIME MACHINE IN A VERY ODD LIBRARY. THEY DISCOVERED THAT BOOKS FROM THE LIBRARY COULD POWER THE MACHINE AND TRANSPORT THEM TO DIFFERENT PLACES AND TIMES. IN THIS ADVENTURE, MIA, BEN, AND SAM MEET GEORGE WASHINGTON!

THIS IS THE TEAM TIME MACHINE LIBRARY. TO VISIT ANY PLACE AND TIME, ALL YOU NEED TO DO IS PLACE A BOOK IN THE TIME MACHINE AND PULL THE HANDLE!

CHAPTER 2: INTO THE PAST

The library had many books about the American Revolution. But would there be a whole book about one event? Mia climbed up the wooden ladder to the top shelf.

"There!" She saw a book called *Washington Crosses the Delaware.* "Everybody ready?"

Mia placed the book from the shelf in the time machine and pulled the handle. The room started to shake. She gripped the ladder, and Ben and Sam held on to the bookshelves. Finally, the movement stopped. They stepped out of a tent into an army camp in Pennsylvania!

WE WENT BACK IN TIME TO CHRISTMAS DAY, DECEMBER 25, 1776. THAT'S THE DAY GEORGE WASHINGTON TOOK HIS SOLDIERS OVER THE DELAWARE RIVER AND MARCHED TO TRENTON, NEW JERSEY.

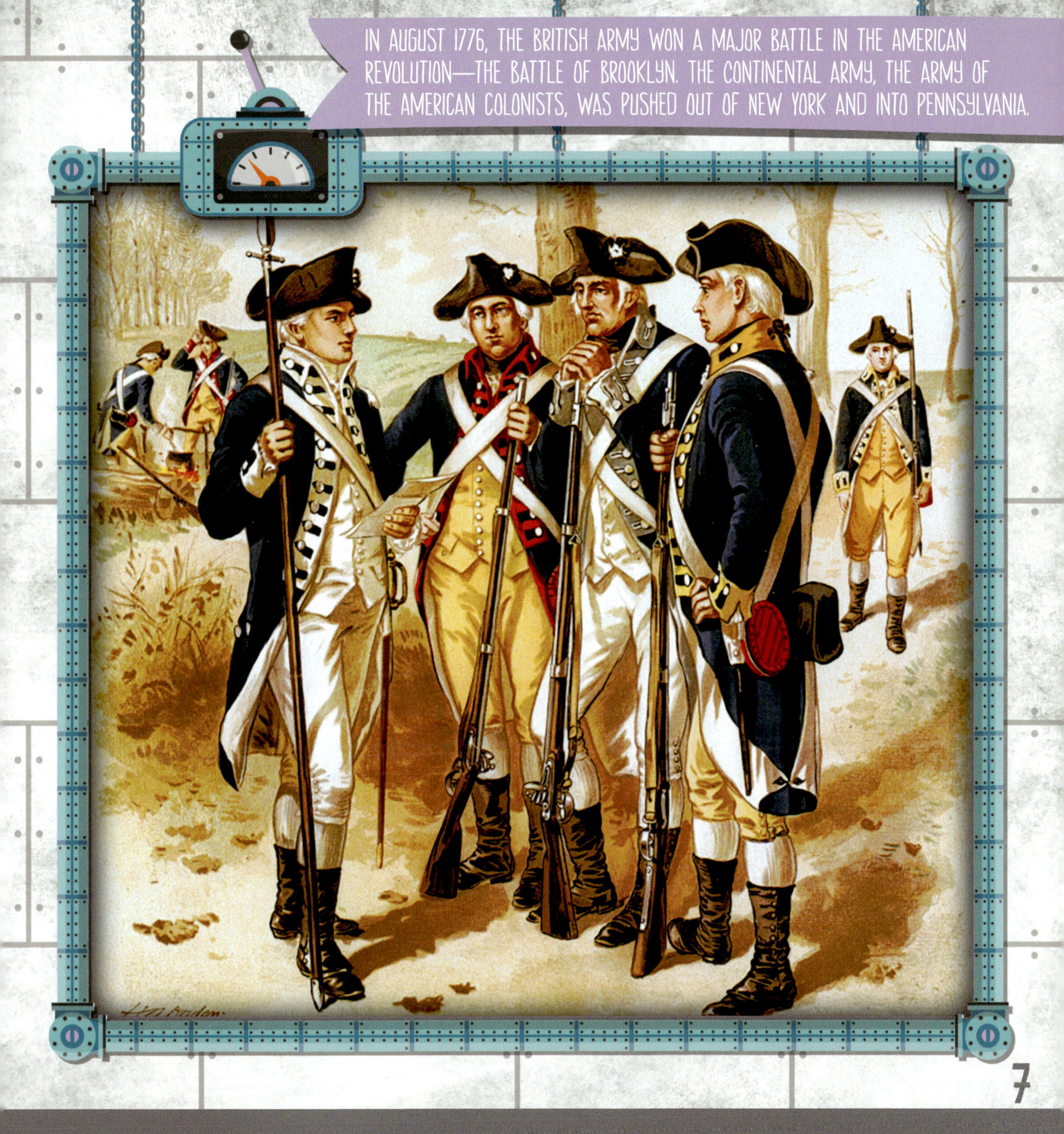

IN AUGUST 1776, THE BRITISH ARMY WON A MAJOR BATTLE IN THE AMERICAN REVOLUTION—THE BATTLE OF BROOKLYN. THE CONTINENTAL ARMY, THE ARMY OF THE AMERICAN COLONISTS, WAS PUSHED OUT OF NEW YORK AND INTO PENNSYLVANIA.

CHAPTER 3: THE CONTINENTAL ARMY

The team knew British soldiers wore red uniforms. Most of the soldiers in this camp wore brown, so they were Continental soldiers.

During the American Revolution, there were two main groups of American soldiers. Regular citizens made up the militia. They fought to protect communities when needed. Some militia promised to be ready at a moment's notice. They were called "minutemen."

The Continental Congress, a group of colonial leaders, created the Continental army in June 1775. It was the first US army. Many of the soldiers were teenagers!

OUR BOOK SAYS THE CONTINENTAL CONGRESS FIRST MET IN 1774 BECAUSE COLONISTS WERE ANGRY WITH BRITISH TAXES AND OTHER LAWS. AFTER FORMING THE CONTINENTAL ARMY, THEY NAMED GEORGE WASHINGTON ITS COMMANDER.

AT FIRST, CONTINENTAL ARMY SOLDIERS WERE TOLD TO WEAR BROWN UNIFORMS. IN LATER YEARS, THEY WORE BLUE. SOLDIERS OFTEN WEREN'T DRESSED CORRECTLY, THOUGH!

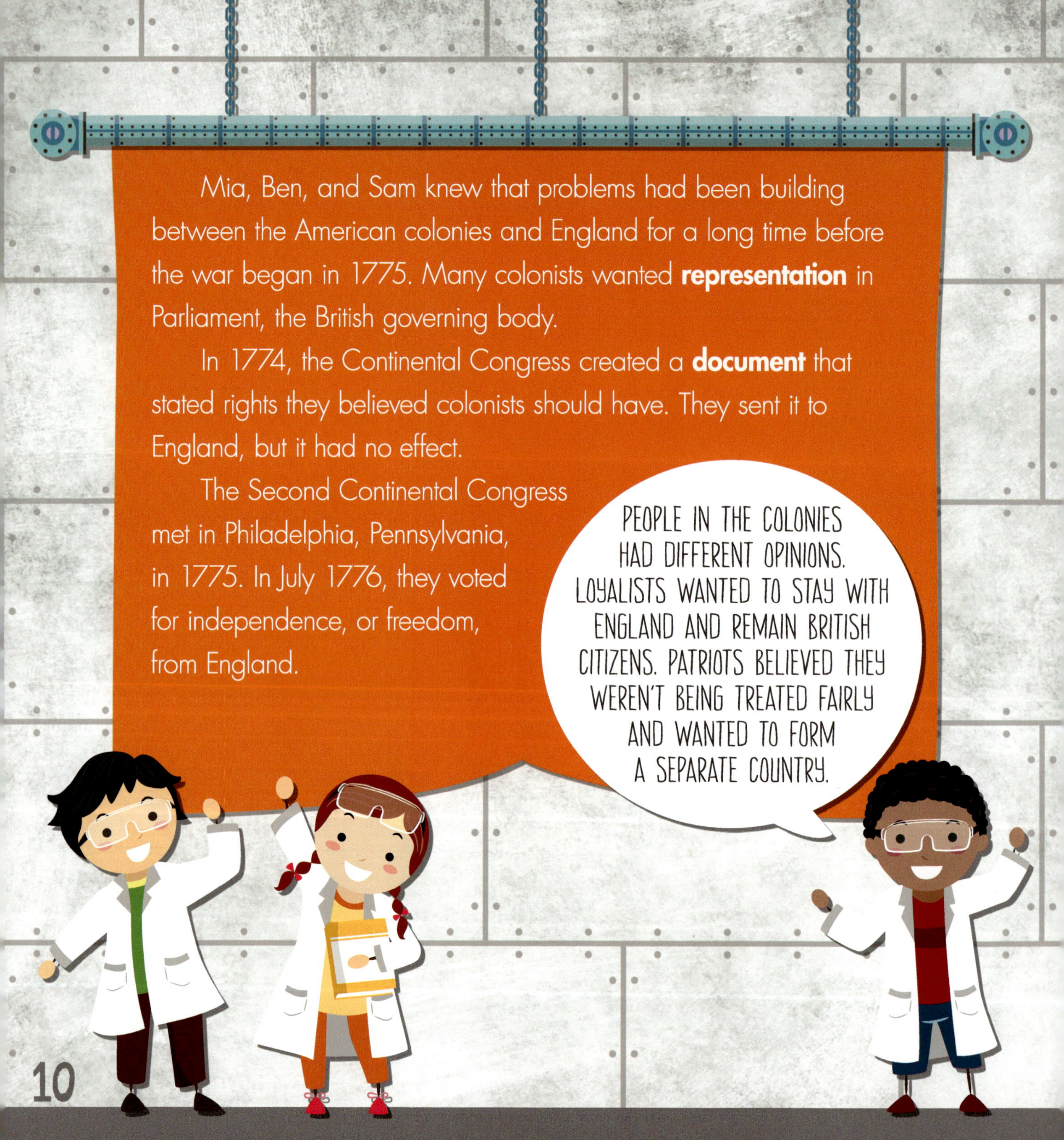

Mia, Ben, and Sam knew that problems had been building between the American colonies and England for a long time before the war began in 1775. Many colonists wanted **representation** in Parliament, the British governing body.

In 1774, the Continental Congress created a **document** that stated rights they believed colonists should have. They sent it to England, but it had no effect.

The Second Continental Congress met in Philadelphia, Pennsylvania, in 1775. In July 1776, they voted for independence, or freedom, from England.

THE BATTLES OF LEXINGTON AND CONCORD IN MASSACHUSETTS, WHICH TOOK PLACE ON APRIL 19, 1775, WERE THE FIRST REAL BATTLES OF THE AMERICAN REVOLUTION.

CHAPTER 4: GENERAL GEORGE WASHINGTON

"There's President George Washington!" shouted Mia.

"Not yet! He's still *General* Washington," Sam reminded her.

The members of the team met a boy about their age named William. He was carrying water to the soldiers. He told them how the army had ended up there.

For several months, the Continental army had been beaten in battles. They had lost important locations, including New York City. Many people in the colonies and in England believed Washington's army couldn't win the war. **Morale** was low.

WILLIAM SAID THE CONTINENTAL ARMY DIDN'T HAVE ENOUGH SUPPLIES. THEY OFTEN DIDN'T HAVE ENOUGH UNIFORMS OR FOOD. THEY WEREN'T PAID WELL, EITHER!

GEORGE WASHINGTON WAS BORN ON FEBRUARY 22, 1732. HIS MILITARY CAREER BEGAN WITH THE VIRGINIA MILITIA DURING THE FRENCH AND INDIAN WAR (1754–1763).

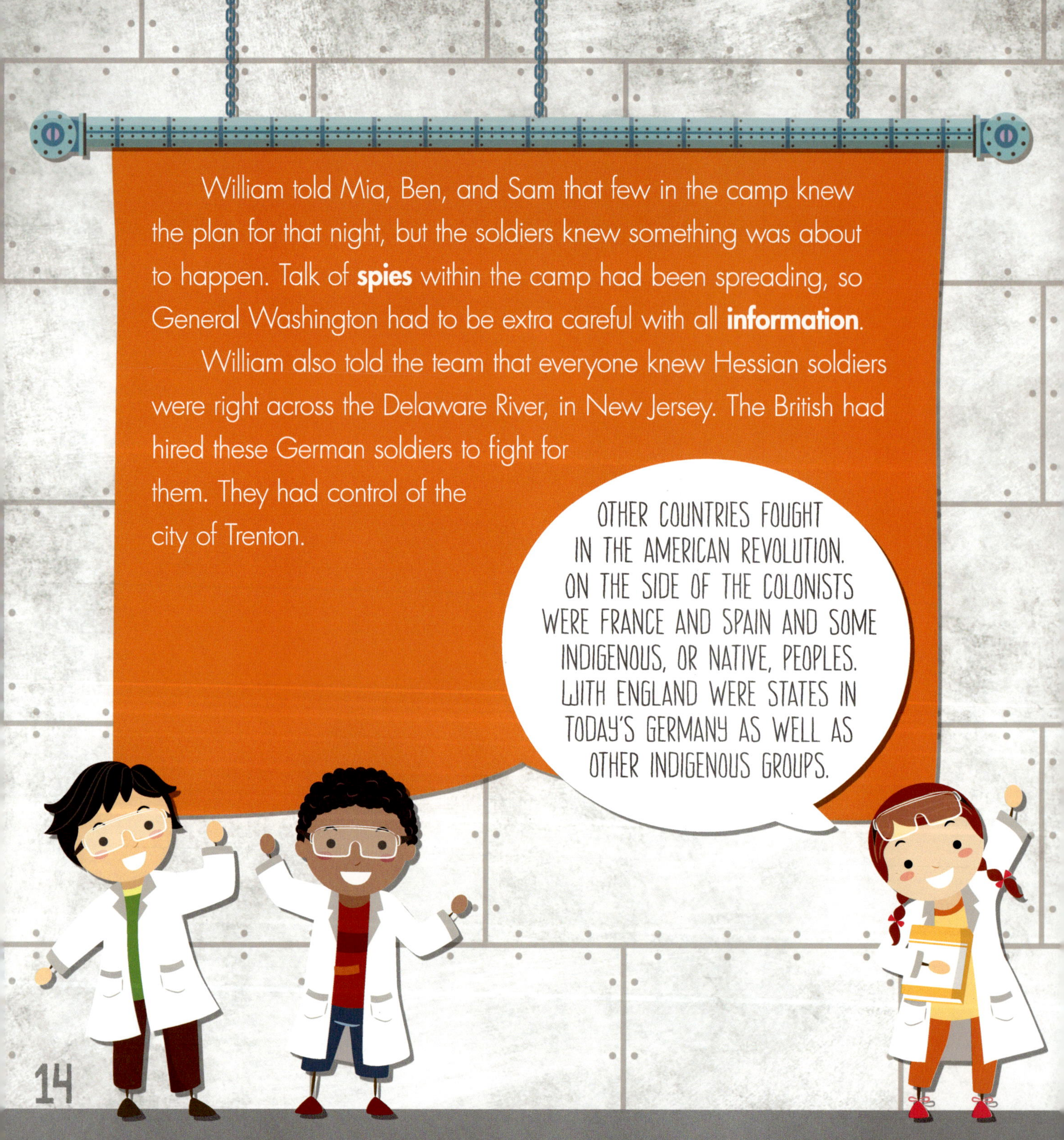

William told Mia, Ben, and Sam that few in the camp knew the plan for that night, but the soldiers knew something was about to happen. Talk of **spies** within the camp had been spreading, so General Washington had to be extra careful with all **information**.

William also told the team that everyone knew Hessian soldiers were right across the Delaware River, in New Jersey. The British had hired these German soldiers to fight for them. They had control of the city of Trenton.

ABOUT 30,000 HESSIAN SOLDIERS FOUGHT IN THE AMERICAN REVOLUTION. THEY WERE FROM THE GERMAN STATE CALLED HESSE-KASSEL.

CHAPTER 5: ON THE MOVE!

Around 11:00 p.m., the Continental soldiers started to move. The wintry weather wasn't getting better. In fact, the river was half frozen. Mia, Ben, and Sam located General Washington and stayed close. They figured if they stuck by him, they wouldn't miss anything!

The army split into three and took off in boats from different locations. Many of those boats came from a local iron company, and they could carry a lot of weight. Washington led about 2,400 soldiers across the river.

THE BOATS WE TOOK ACROSS THE DELAWARE HAD FLAT BOTTOMS, SO THEY COULD FIT A LOT OF MEN. BUT THE WATER WAS REALLY CHOPPY—WE HAD TO SIT INSIDE THE BOATS AND HANG ON!

MANY OF THE BOATS USED BY WASHINGTON'S FORCE WERE CALLED DURHAM BOATS. THEY WERE MADE TO CARRY GOODS UP TO ABOUT 15 TONS (13.6 MT). SO, A COUPLE OF **STOWAWAYS** DIDN'T MAKE A DIFFERENCE!

It was hard to move through the water! The ice and wind whipped at the faces of the team, and they shivered in the cold along with the soldiers. Yet, General Washington led the men forward.

Sam, Ben, and Mia, along with many Continental soldiers, landed on the other side of the Delaware River. But less than half the soldiers had made it across! About 3,000 men failed to reach the meeting place. The remaining force formed two rows and prepared for the attack.

MONUMENT MARKING WHERE WASHINGTON CROSSED THE DELAWARE

EMANUEL LEUTZE'S FAMOUS 1851 PAINTING *WASHINGTON CROSSING THE DELAWARE* DOESN'T SHOW THINGS AS THEY ACTUALLY HAPPENED. FOR EXAMPLE, GEORGE WASHINGTON WASN'T THAT OLD WHEN THE CONTINENTAL ARMY CROSSED THE DELAWARE!

CHAPTER 6: THE BATTLE OF TRENTON

It was about 8:00 a.m. on December 26 when General Washington's army reached Trenton, New Jersey. It wasn't totally a surprise attack. However, the Hessians didn't think the Patriot force was a real **threat**. Ben, Mia, and Sam watched as sleepy German soldiers struggled to find their guns and prepare their forces to fight back. The battle didn't take long.

The Continental army soon won with few **casualties** on either side. By 9:30 a.m., the town was surrounded. Washington's army had captured 1,000 men.

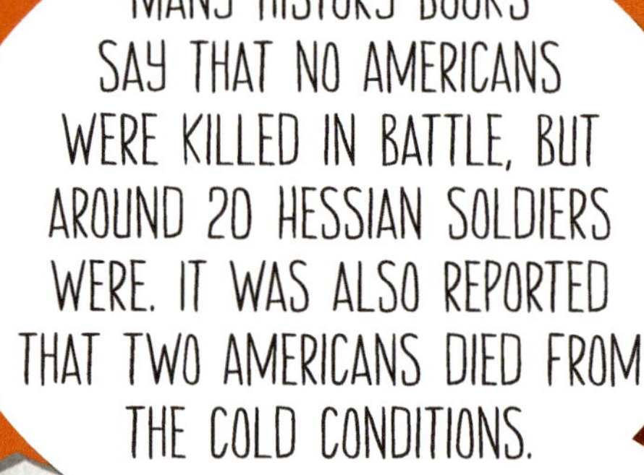

HESSIAN COLONEL JOHANN RALL, COMMANDER OF THE HESSIAN TROOPS, WAS WOUNDED IN THE BATTLE AND DIED THE NEXT DAY.

CHAPTER 7: RECROSSING THE DELAWARE

The Battle of Trenton was won! However, General Washington still didn't have most of his army. They were on the other side of the Delaware River. Without enough soldiers to hold Trenton, Washington withdrew his force and recrossed the water to meet up with the remainder of his men. The army took the captured Hessians with them.

The team saw William again when they returned with the Continental army to the camp. He was happy about the victory. Soldiers played music to celebrate!

WILLIAM TOLD US THAT SOLDIERS IN THE CAMP LIVE BY THE SOUND OF MUSIC. IN THE MORNING, THEY GET UP TO THE SOUND OF THE FIFE AND DRUMS. WHEN THEY'RE MARCHING, THE MUSIC TELLS THEM WHERE TO GO!

SOME IN THE CONTINENTAL ARMY PLAYED A SMALL FLUTE CALLED A FIFE, SHOWN HERE. IT WAS PLAYED FOR ENJOYMENT, BUT ALSO GAVE DIRECTIONS TO SOLDIERS!

CHAPTER 8: ESCAPE TO PRINCETON

A few days later, the Continental army—and Team Time Machine—crossed the Delaware River for a third time. They returned to Trenton, but their forces were driven back by a British army headed by Lord Cornwallis. After the fighting stopped, the two forces set up camp.

Under Washington's order, the Continental army snuck out of their camp and escaped from the British in the middle of the night. They marched on to Princeton, capturing it on January 3, 1777.

HISTORY BOOKS SAY THAT THE BATTLES OF TRENTON AND PRINCETON WERE IMPORTANT BECAUSE THEY ENDED THE STRING OF BRITISH VICTORIES AND RAISED AMERICAN MORALE. WASHINGTON PROVED HIMSELF TO BE A SMART LEADER.

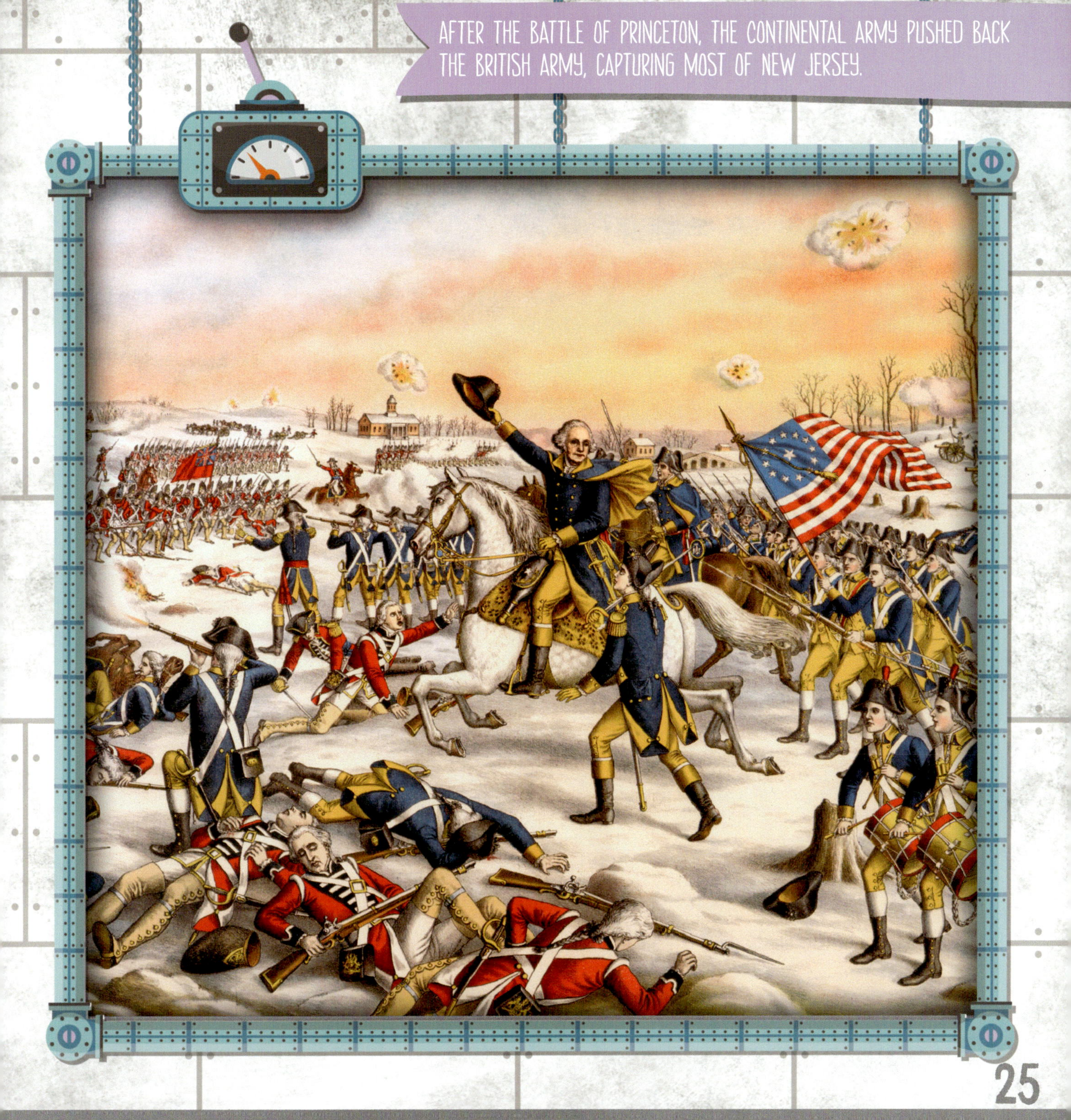
AFTER THE BATTLE OF PRINCETON, THE CONTINENTAL ARMY PUSHED BACK THE BRITISH ARMY, CAPTURING MOST OF NEW JERSEY.

In Princeton, William and Team Time Machine talked over the wonderful turn of events for the Continental army. Suddenly, a tall figure appeared.

"General Washington!" William said. He stood at attention, with his back straight and his arms pinned to his sides. Sam, Ben, and Mia followed William's lead.

General Washington looked tired, but he gave the young people a smile.

"I am much **obliged** to you," he said to everyone. "It is a group of fine fellows we have here."

GENERAL WASHINGTON WENT ON TO LEAD THE CONTINENTAL ARMY TO VICTORY. IN 1781, HE LED A RISKY MARCH SOUTH TO SURROUND LORD CORNWALLIS'S ARMY AT YORKTOWN, VIRGINIA. IT WAS THE LAST MAJOR BATTLE OF THE WAR.

CHAPTER 9: HOME AGAIN

With the American victory in sight, Mia, Ben, and Sam knew it was time to go home. Strangely, they found the tent they came through in Pennsylvania in the army camp in New Jersey—and inside was the library! Sam took the book out of the time machine and placed it back on the shelf.

Back in their own time, the team let out a deep breath.

"Can you believe all that happened?" asked Sam.

Mia answered, "It seems like a dream!"

"I can't wait to go back to Trenton with Mom!" said Ben.

THERE'S MORE TO LEARN ABOUT THIS AND OTHER EVENTS OF THE AMERICAN REVOLUTION. VISIT THE LIBRARY—YOU MAY FIND YOUR OWN TIME MACHINE!

EVERY YEAR, **REENACTORS** SET OUT TOGETHER TO CROSS THE DELAWARE ON CHRISTMAS DAY. THEY DRESS UP AS GEORGE WASHINGTON AND OTHER SOLDIERS OF THE CONTINENTAL ARMY.

casualty: someone who has been hurt or killed

document: a formal or official piece of writing

Electoral College: a group of people chosen from each US state who meet to elect the president and vice president based on the votes of all the people in each state

information: knowledge about something

morale: the mental and emotional condition of a group of people

obliged: very grateful

reenactor: one who repeats events that already happened, often for entertainment

representation: a person or group that speaks or acts for or in support of another person or group

revolution: a movement to overthrow an established government

spy: a person who tries secretly to get information about a country or organization for another country or organization

stowaway: someone who hides on a ship in order to travel without being seen

threat: something likely to cause harm

unanimously: with agreement by everyone

FOR MORE INFORMATION

BOOKS

Axelrod, Alan. *The Revolutionary War: 1775 – 1783.* New York, NY: Abbeville Kids, 2016.

Kravitz, Danny. *The Untold Story of Washington's Surprise Attack: The Daring Crossing of the Delaware River.* North Mankato, MN: Compass Point Books, 2015.

Landau, Elaine. *General Washington Crosses the Delaware: Would You Join the American Revolution?* Berkeley Heights, NJ: Enslow Elementary, 2015.

WEBSITES

American Revolution
www.ducksters.com/history/american_revolution.php
Learn about what caused the American Revolution and more about the people who took part.

George Washington's Mount Vernon: For Students
www.mountvernon.org/education/for-students/
Find out more about George Washington—commander of the Continental army and first president of the United States.

INDEX